THE LISTED STRUCTURES
IN WEST NORWOOD CEMETERY

Geoffrey Manning

NORWOOD SOCIETY

Memorials in West Norwood Cemetery

A record of structures listed by the
Department of the Environment as of special
architectural or historic interest.

Geoffrey Manning

Copyright © 1989 by the Norwood Society

Design and graphics Mike Conrad

Typesetting Delwest Graphics

Artwork Javed Khan

Published by the Norwood Society 1989

Printed by Tadberry Evedale Ltd.

ISBN 0 9515384 0 3

WEST NORWOOD CEMETERY

The history of West Norwood Cemetery dates from the reign of William IV when alternatives to the overcrowded churchyards of London had to be found urgently. Eight private cemetery companies were authorised by Acts of Parliament to establish burial grounds in the country then immediately surrounding London. The second of these companies, the South Metropolitan Cemetery Company, was incorporated in 1836 and acquired some 40 acres of land next to the hamlet of Norwood in the southernmost part of the parish of Lambeth on what had been part of Lord Chancellor Thurlow's extensive estate in South London. The company's architect (and one of the directors) was William Tite, later Sir William, president of the Royal Institute of British Architects and perhaps best known for his Royal Exchange. He laid out the cemetery to an informal pattern taking advantage of the undulating site, built two chapels, an office, an entrance arch and surrounded it all with high brick walls and cast iron railings. The first burial took place on 12 December 1837. Cremation was introduced in 1915.

The cemetery and its buildings suffered bomb damage during the 1939-45 war, and by the 1960's it was virtually full and had become neglected and overgrown. It was purchased by the London Borough of Lambeth in 1966 for £6000, and the Council's intention was to continue with the cremation service and to turn the grounds into a memorial park where people could relax in tranquil surroundings and enjoy what had been described at the time as both an 'ecological reservoir and an 'extremely attractive open air history book'. The Local Authority Cemetery Order 1977 varied the right of burial in perpetuity, enabling the considerable areas of older graves to be re-used for burials.

Thus the cemetery is fully operational again and now comprises interesting contrasts of old and new.

The cemetery, together with the adjoining parish church and other nearby buildings, was designated a Conservation Area in 1978 and was subsequently recognised by the Secretary of State for the Environment as 'outstanding' under the then current terminology.

The cemetery entrance arches and gates, and the walls, iron fences, railings, gate piers and gates on the west and south sides, and the walls and railings on the Robson Road frontage are designated as buildings of special architectural or historic interest, grade II. Within the cemetery there are seven tombs listed grade II* and 37 others listed grade II. They are set out below, the preceding number corresponds to the number on the plan. Two graves no longer survive: that of John Garrett (No. 19) which was an unusual wooden gothic memorial of 1881; and that of Sir William Cubitt (died 1861), former president of the Institution of Civil Engineers who supervised the erection of the Crystal Palace in Hyde Park (No. 15). Most of the other listed tombs are in varying stages of decay.

Of Tite's original buildings, the surrounding wall and iron railings survive, together with the entrance arch (RIGHT). His episcopal chapel, in a style reminiscent of Kings College Chapel, was war damaged and demolished in 1955 by the Company and replaced by a walled rose garden. The catacombs are underneath. The smaller dissenters' chapel was also demolished and replaced by the present unremarkable crematorium in about 1960. The archway is inscribed 'South Metropolitan Cemetery Incorporated AD MDCCCXXXVI' with shields bearing the arms of the dioceses of Canterbury and Winchester. Above the pedestrian entrance to the right is carved a crown and scroll inscribed 'Deus Deo' and on the inner side the date 1837. The offices behind the arch to the right are not the original; these were rebuilt in 1936 and again in 1952.

1 J W EVERIDGE – a handsome example of the mixed renaissance style of the period, comprising principally a Jacobean arch and segmental pediment, richly ornamented with cherubs etc. It has been given the date 1868 although that is clearly many years before J W Everidge's death. There is a record of a burial of an Everidge in 1868 in another part of the cemetery, and who was later transferred to this grave; perhaps the monument was transferred too.

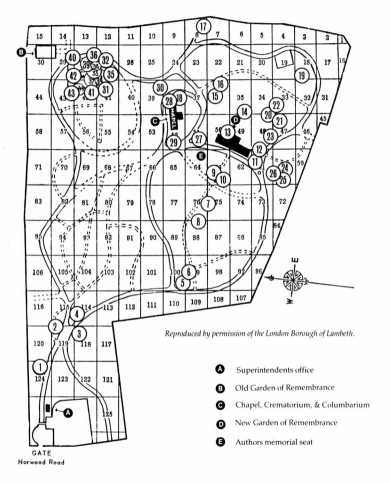

Reproduced by permission of the London Borough of Lambeth.

A Superintendents office
B Old Garden of Remembrance
C Chapel, Crematorium, & Columbarium
D New Garden of Remembrance
E Authors memorial seat

1 Tomb of J W Everidge (1868) (II)
2 Tomb of Alfred Longsdon (d.1893) (II)
3 Tomb of John Britton (1857) (II*)
4 Tomb of J W Gilbart (d.1863) (II)
5 Tomb of Dr. Gideon Mantell (d.1852) (II*)
6 Tomb of Sir Henry Bessemer (d.1898) (II)
7 Tomb of Capt. Wimble (d.1851) (II)
8 Tomb of Pond family (dated 1881) (II)
9 Tomb of Thomas de la Garde Grissell (d.1847) (II)
10 Tomb of Alexander Berens (1858) (II*)
11 Tomb of Dr. William Marsden (d.1867) (II)
12 Tomb of Harris family (mid C19) (II)
13 Tomb of George Dodd (1865) (II)
14 Tomb of Nicholson family (1857) (II)
15 Tomb of Sir William Cubitt (d.1861) (II)
16 Tomb of Sir Henry Doulton (1897) (II)
17 Tomb of Mrs. Anne Farrow (d.1854) (II)
18 Tomb of Sir Henry Tate (1890) (II*)
19 Tomb of John Garrett (d.1881) (II)
20 Tomb of William Crane (d.1856) (II)
21 Tomb of John Stevens (d.1861) (II)
22 Tomb of Elizabeth Burgess (d.1855) (II*)
23 Tomb of Thomas Cubitt (d.1855) (II)
24 Tomb of Rev. William Punshon (d.1881) (II)
25 Tomb of Mrs. Alice Moffat (d.1847) (II)
26 Tomb of Mrs. Ann Joyce (1839) (II)
27 Tomb of Capper family (c.1842) (II)
28 Tomb of Rev. Charles Spurgeon (d.1892) (II)
29 Tomb of Christopher Gabriel (d.1873) (II)

30 Tomb of Benjamin Colls (d.1878) (II)
31 Mortuary chapel in Greek cemetery (c.1872) (II*)
32 Tomb of Eustratios Ralli (c.1875) (II)
33 Tomb of Skvaitch (II)
34 Tomb of P A Ralli family (late C19) (II)
35 Tomb of Vlasto family (late C19) (II)
36 Tomb of Spartali (later C19) (II)
37 Tomb of Rodocanachi family (II)
38 Tomb of T E Schilizzi (1872) (II)
39 Tomb of John Peter Ralli (d.1863) (II*)
40 Tomb of Balli (late C19) (II)
41 Tomb of Mavrogordato (1890) (II)
42 Tomb of P A Argenti (late C19) (II)
43 Tomb of Michalinos family (1911) (II)
44 Tomb of Stephen Schilizzi (1908) (II)

Among other graves of interest
(Numbers refer to squares on the map)

48   Henry Beaufoy (1786-1851) – Educational philanthropist – built and endowed Lambeth Ragged Schools.

63   Mrs Isabella Beeton (1836-65) – Authoress of "Mrs Beeton's Book of Household Management" – first published in 1861.

99   Charles Bravo (1846-76) – The poison victim of one of the most celebrated unpunished Victorian crimes.

35   Thomas Lynn Bristowe (1833-92) – First MP for Norwood. He secured Brockwell Park for the public but died at the formal opening.

52   William Edgar (1791-1869) – Established Swan & Edgar's in Piccadilly 1834.

61   Sir James Hannen (1821-94) – Presided over the Parnell enquiry 1888.

38   John Lawson Johnstone (1839-1900) – "Mr Bovril".

124   Thomas King (1835-88) – Prizefighter – Champion of England in 1862.

124   Edmund Distim Maddick CBE FRCS (died 1939) – Surgeon – built the Scala Theatre 1905 – Director of Kinematography in World War I.

81   Augustus Manns (1823-1907) – Director of Music at Crystal Palace for 40 years.

124   Sir Hiram Stevens Maxim (1840-1916) – Prolific inventor – including the Maxim Gun.

22   Sir William Francis Napier (1785-1860) – Soldier and historian – fought under Moore and Wellington in the Peninsular War.

95   Col John Cyril Porte (1884-1919) – Inventor of the flying boat.

23   Baron Paul Julius de Reuter (1816-99) – Founder of the famous press agency.

–   Sir William Tite (1798-1873) – Architect of the cemetery and of The Royal Exchange – president of the RIBA – buried in the Catacombs.

Grade II Buildings of special interest.
Grade II* Buildings of particular importance.

2 Alfred LONGSDON (d.1893) and Elizabeth Longsdon (d. 1892) of Denmark Hill. Their mausoleum is of Portland stone ashlar, surmounted by a tall dome.

3 John BRITTON (1771-1857) was the most distinguished medieval antiquary of the early 19th century; he was the father of the study of the English cathedrals on which he published many books. His monument, a single rough cut rectangular block of brown granite set on end and over 10'high, is by George Godwin (1803-1887) – called the father of architectural journalism – who was editor of the Builder from 1844 to 1883.

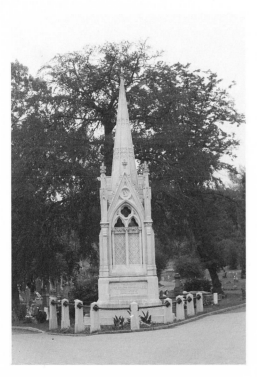

4 James GILBART (1794-1863) wrote the classic book on banking and was for many years manager of the London Westminster Bank. There are remarkable eulogies to his worth inscribed on the monument, and a carved squirrel on a gable is apposite. William Tite was also architect to the Bank and this gothic monument is attributed to him. It takes the form of a square 'Belfry' with gables over open windows surmounted by a banded spire. It is admirably maintained by subventions from private sources.

5 Dr. Gideon MANTELL (1790-1852) was a Sussex doctor who discovered fossil teeth in a quarry near Cuckfield which he interpreted as those of a prehistoric creature he called the iguanadon. Later, more complete discoveries confirmed the remarkable accuracy of his predicted iguanadon structure. His dinosaur discoveries were the basis of the models of prehistoric creatures created for the Crystal Palace by Waterhouse Hawkins. His monument is probably by Eamon Wilds who was the architect for much of Regency Brighton. An interesting aspect of the design was a planting of a cypress assymetrically within the grave; the tree was toppled in the hurricane of October 1987 and had to be cut back to a stump for safety reasons. Little remains of the original surrounding iron rail. Restoration is awaited at the time of publication.

6 Sir Henry BESSEMER FRS (b. 1813.) A tomb listed principally because of the historic importance of Sir Henry, a prolific inventor. He took out 114 patents but is most famous for his process for converting pig iron into steel. He lived from 1863 on Demark Hill at what is now the corner of Sunray Avenue running down to the present James Allen school, a large estate which included a deer park, a model farm and an observatory with what was at the time the world's 2nd largest telescope. He died on 15.3.1898.

7 Capt. John WIMBLE (d. 1851 aged 54) has been joined by his wife who shared some of his adventures during 34 years at sea. On the sides of the tomb are depicted ships and shipwrecks and it is surmounted by a carved merchantman, now dismasted. After he left the sea, Capt. Wimble retired to Upper Tulse Hill.

8 The POND family mausoleum contains among others Christopher Pond (1826 - 1881), a wine merchant who built the Criterion Theatre and Restaurant, and who helped to organise the visit of the first English cricket team to Australia in 1861. His home was at The Cedars, Herne Hill.

9 Thomas De La Garde GRISSELL's tomb is of early Victorian design made of stucco and cast iron, with traceried inscription panels. Nothing remains of what were very fine wrought iron railings surrounding the tomb. Grissell lived at Stockwell Common and died in 1847 aged 69. The tomb holds his wife and other members of the family and commemorates two sons who both served with the Bengal Native Infantry. He was a Fellow of the Society of Antiquaries of London.

10 Alexander BERENS, linen draper of St. Paul's Churchyard, died on 15 April 1860, aged 63, at his home at Raleigh Hall, Brixton Rise. His tomb is arguably the finest in the cemetery. It was designed by Edward M Barry in medieval Italian Style and erected in 1858 at a cost said to be £1500. The base is of red polished granite, with marble superstructure excepting the Portland stone sculptured sections. The doors and other bronze work were manufactured by Potter who also made the original surrounding railings. The new testament and other sculptures are by Thomas Earp, with an evangelist at each corner. A surrounding band of Minton tiles carries the Berens crest and a device formed by the letter B alternately.

An illustration in the Builder of November 1858 showed its original magnificence; now it is sadly neglected, with roof cracked and tree growing from it, the stone carvings flaking and doors and ironwork gone.

11 Dr. William MARSDEN (d. 1857) founder of the Royal Free Hospital and the Royal Marsden Cancer Hospital is commemorated by a Regency-style monument. The elegant urn that surmounted the circular column has been lost.

12 The mausoleum to Edith HARRIS (d. 1867) and others may date back to 1840. It is in the neo-classical style ((27) is another, perhaps better, example) with bare walls supported on a massive plinth with vermiculated rustication, and a 'bat's ear' at each corner of the roof.

13 is a fine example of the medieval Italian influence of High Victorian architecture, designed by Thomas Allom (1804-72) who also designed the Ladbroke Grove estate in North Kensington. It commemorates George DODD (d. 1864) who was MP for Maidstone 1841-53. The white marble mausoleum suffered bomb damage and is in a poor state of repair.

14 The NICHOLSON family tomb is said to be listed solely on account of the quality of the lettering. Is it really that good?

17 A delicate wrought and cast iron monument which some how so far has survived vandalism and rust. It commemorates Mrs Ann FARROW (d. 1854). The monument is a remarkable example of the fearless use of new materials by the Victorians.

16 Sir Henry DOULTON, the potter and inventor of Doultonware whose factory was on the river at Lambeth, died in 1897. He lived at Woodlands, Streatham Park Estate, near Tooting Bec Common. His mausoleum is a handsome composition in red brick and terra cotta, attributed to R. Stark Wilkinson, who designed the Doulton Pottery on Albert Embankment. The sculpture in Doultonware over the door may be by George Tinworth, the chief sculptor for Doulton's who himself is buried in

the cemetery. There were two splendid Doulton vases inside which have been stolen. The mausoleum also commemorates Henry Lewis Doulton, his son and chairman of Doulton's (d. 1930).

18 Similar to (16), this mausoleum is more sensitively detailed and shows Victorian terra cotta at its best. It commemorates Sir Henry TATE, art collector and philanthropist, who died in 1899. It was designed by S.R.J.Smith who had done much work for Sir Henry including the Tate Gallery and libraries which Sir Henry had presented to Lambeth. Tate lived at Park Hill, Streatham Common North, having made his fortune in Liverpool by developing sugar cube and refining processes.

20 The slab is all that remains of the tomb of William CRANE (d.1856) and others of his family. It was once surmounted by a tall cross of pink granite with foliated arms and continuous vine trails to the stem. A bronze inscription tablet named the members of the family in classical trajanic lettering. It was said to be a remarkable example of the style of design associated with Sir Henry Cole's group at the South Kensington Museum.

22 William BURGESS was one of the most famous Victorian Gothic architects, perhaps best known for his rebuilding of Cardiff Castle and Castell Coch in South Wales. His extraordinary house in Melbury Road, Kensington, is preserved as a museum. This sarcophagus he designed for his mother Elizabeth (d.1855) and was uncharacteristically simple; just grey stone with on the lid a carved cross looped into a love knot. His father Alfred,

who died when 90, is also in the tomb — he was a leading civil engineer of his day building lighthouses, docks, roads and sewers; Bazalgette was his junior partner. William Burgess died in 1881 and also lies in the tomb.

21 The large obelisk is a memorial to John STEVENS, an engineer who lived at Clapham Common. He was inventor and patentee of semaphore signals, and the railway engineering company he founded was in Southwark Bridge Road. He died 1861. The obelisk is of grey granite with incised decorations, by Anderson and McKenzie of Aberdeen.

23 Thomas CUBITT (d.1855) is said to be the father of the modern contracting industry – the first builder to employ all tradesmen on a permanent wage basis. He created most of Belgravia, Pimlico and Clapham Park. He was adviser to Queen Victoria and Prince Albert, personally supervising the alterations to Osborne House for them. He refused all honours (but his brother William – not the William Cubitt of (15) – became Lord Mayor and was knighted and his son became Baron Ashcombe in 1892). The tomb is a ten ton slab of granite surrounded by a holly hedge.

24 This is a fine High Victorian Gothic monument carved by J Rogerson of Liverpool, and commemorating the Rev. William Morley PUNSHON (d.1881), a Wesleyan minister who lived in Brixton Rise.

25 The early Victorian Gothic monument of Mrs. Alice MOFFAT (d. 1847) had an open work trefoiled arcade of stucco and iron of which some only of its iron supports survive.

28 The funeral of the Reverend Charles Haddon SPURGEON (d. 31.1.1892) was reported to have attracted more mourners than any other funeral in the cemetery's history. He was a spell-binding preacher whose home was off Beulah Hill in Upper Norwood. The monument is a massive and rhetorical sarcophagus of grey granite with a rather coarse bust, and is listed for its historical rather than artistic significance.

26 The Regency style monument with a well-carved acanthus frieze (by Carlini) is one of the earliest in the cemetery. It marks the tomb of Mrs. Ann JOYCE who died in 1839 aged 24, her son aged 18 months and her husband who too died young.

27 Not dissimilar to the Harris mausoleum (no. 12), this temple-shaped mausoleum originally for Mrs. Eliza CAPPER (d.1842) is perhaps a more sensitive version.

30 On the headstone of the conventional pink granite tomb to Benjamin COLLS (d. 1878) is an excellent example of Victorian portraiture by little known sculptor, G A Carter.

29 Sited at the point of the cemetery from where fine views across London may be seen is the tomb of Christopher GABRIEL (d. 1873). The carving is by Kelsey and the Regency style iron railings by J Mills of 40 Great Russell Street. Gabriel lived at Norfolk House, Streatham.

THE GREEK CEMETERY

The Oppici tomb is not a listed structure, but is included in this volume as it epitomises with its carvings of the Greek flag and ships what this remarkable cemetery within a cemetery is all about. The Brother-hood of the Greek Community in London acquired the site off the South Metropolitan Cemetery Co. in 1842 and enlarged it in 1872. Members of the Brotherhood were all wealthy merchants and shipowners mostly born in the Greek Islands, who made their fortunes in their adopted land. In this small enclave there are no less than 14 listed tombs and others which should be seriously considered for statutory listing.

31 Most remarkable is the mortuary chapel in memory of Augustus RALLI who died in 1872 whilst at Eton. It is an exceptionally beautiful building in Greek Doric style, of a classical perfection remarkable for the 1870's. The design is attributed to John Oldred Scott (1842-1913) but is so different from his or other architects' work of the time that no one can be sure of the real architect. The ceiling inside the central hall is a richly coffered blue.

34 An elaborate marble sarcophagus in the Italian style marks the tomb of another of the RALLI family.

32 The mausoleum in Greek Doric order commemorating Eustratious RALLI of Chios was designed in about 1875 by E M Barry, completed by T H Vernon, with sculptures by C H and J Mabey of Lambeth (whose tombs lie not far away). The white marble dome has weathered well and altogether it is a distinguished piece of design.

33 The later 19th century SKVAITCH mausoleum is of marble and, like many of the tombs in this cemetery, is not sited to the best advantage. It has a classical chamber with battered sides and pedimented ends.

35 Next to it is another ornately carved sarcophagus commemorating members of the VLASTO family.

36 The classical chamber mausoleum to the SPARTOLI family is of marble and shap granite and can be best seen from the adjacent roadway.

37 The RODOCANACHI sarcophagus is of marble with acroteria at angles. It is later 19th century.

38 The baldechino commemorating T E SCHILIZZI (d.1870) has its fine features obscured by being hemmed in by other tombs.

39 The gabled John Peter RALLI (d. 1863) mausoleum was designed by G E Street in banded granite and white marble, and is an important example of the High Victorian style evolved by Street and others. The workmanship is excellent.

40 The small marble Ionic temple in the north-eastern corner commemorates the BALLI family.

41 The marble tomb of MAVROGORDATO (c 1890) is surrounded by a fine wrought iron screen on a plinth.

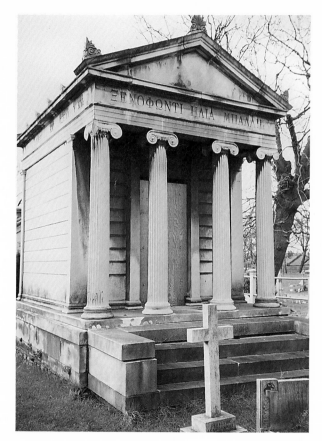